X Over Y

2 Piano Pieces for Contemporary Sight Reading

K.R. Anderson

ISBN 978-0-692-45190-8

Fugue & Fury
PUBLISHING

www.FugueAndFury.com

CONTENTS

HOW TO USE THIS BOOK

This book contains 52 short piano pieces that feature a variety of musical techniques frequently found in modern and contemporary classical compositions. Influences from a wide range of sources and styles can be identified, including: jazz, neoclassicism, serialism, impressionism, postmodernism, romanticism, atonality, counterpoint, and even graphic notation.

For intermediate and advanced pianists wishing to expand their sight reading skills, much of this material has been written to diminish playing by ear and predicting the notes due to stylistic familiarity. Instead, the emphasis is on identifying the visual patterns notated on the written page. Use these exercises as supplementary material to your daily sight reading for a more well-rounded practice.

The exercises are loosely ordered from easier to more difficult, however; this is not a step-by-step practice. Students may simply pick a piece and dive in, subsequently pinpointing which types of passages may need further work in the future. Teachers may also assign pieces which will specifically speak to areas the student requires further experience with. Ultimately, there is no real substitution for simply sitting down to practice the skill of sight reading as much as possible.

Similarly, these pieces can also be used for general technical practice. While many of the passages are physically useful for developing finger dexterity, the aural challenges of this practice encourage proficiency in the navigation of unfamiliar sounds and patterns.

ADDITIONAL NOTES

TEMPO
Precise metronome timings have been provided for each exercise, but for sight reading purposes, strict adherence is not necessary. Choose a tempo that allows completion of the exercise without excessive stops or pauses.

PEDALING
Except when explicitly specified, the pianist may pedal as needed. Or if desired, pedaling may also be eliminated entirely in order to simplify the sight reading exercise.

FINGERINGS
Suggested fingerings have been provided for many of the more intricate passages, however; they are only guidelines. Don't hesitate to use whatever fingerings feel the most comfortable, or that facilitate the best performance.

SECONDS IN TIME

K.R. ANDERSON

I'M FEELING NICE

K.R. ANDERSON

ONE AT A TIME

K.R. ANDERSON

BEHIND THE TIMES

K.R. ANDERSON

FIVE BY 5

K.R. ANDERSON

ROUNDABOUT

K.R. ANDERSON

CONTRAPTION

K.R. ANDERSON

REFLECTION

K.R. ANDERSON

CROSSING THE LINE

K.R. ANDERSON

CAN'T KEEP ME IN D

K.R. ANDERSON

INTO THE SWING OF THINGS

K.R. ANDERSON

SOLSTICE NIGHT

K.R. ANDERSON

QUAVERLY

K.R. ANDERSON

TOGETHER FOREVER

K.R. ANDERSON

THERE'S ALWAYS ONE

K.R. ANDERSON

LABORIOUS

K.R. ANDERSON

STEADY, NOW

K.R. ANDERSON

ROUNDING 50

K.R. ANDERSON

HAPPY UNBIRTHDAY

K.R. ANDERSON

SUSTAINABLE

K.R. ANDERSON

LUMBERFUL

K.R. ANDERSON

A HYMN FOR NONEXISTENCE

K.R. ANDERSON

WOOLGATHERING

K.R. ANDERSON

OVER THE CLEF

K.R. ANDERSON

325

K.R. ANDERSON

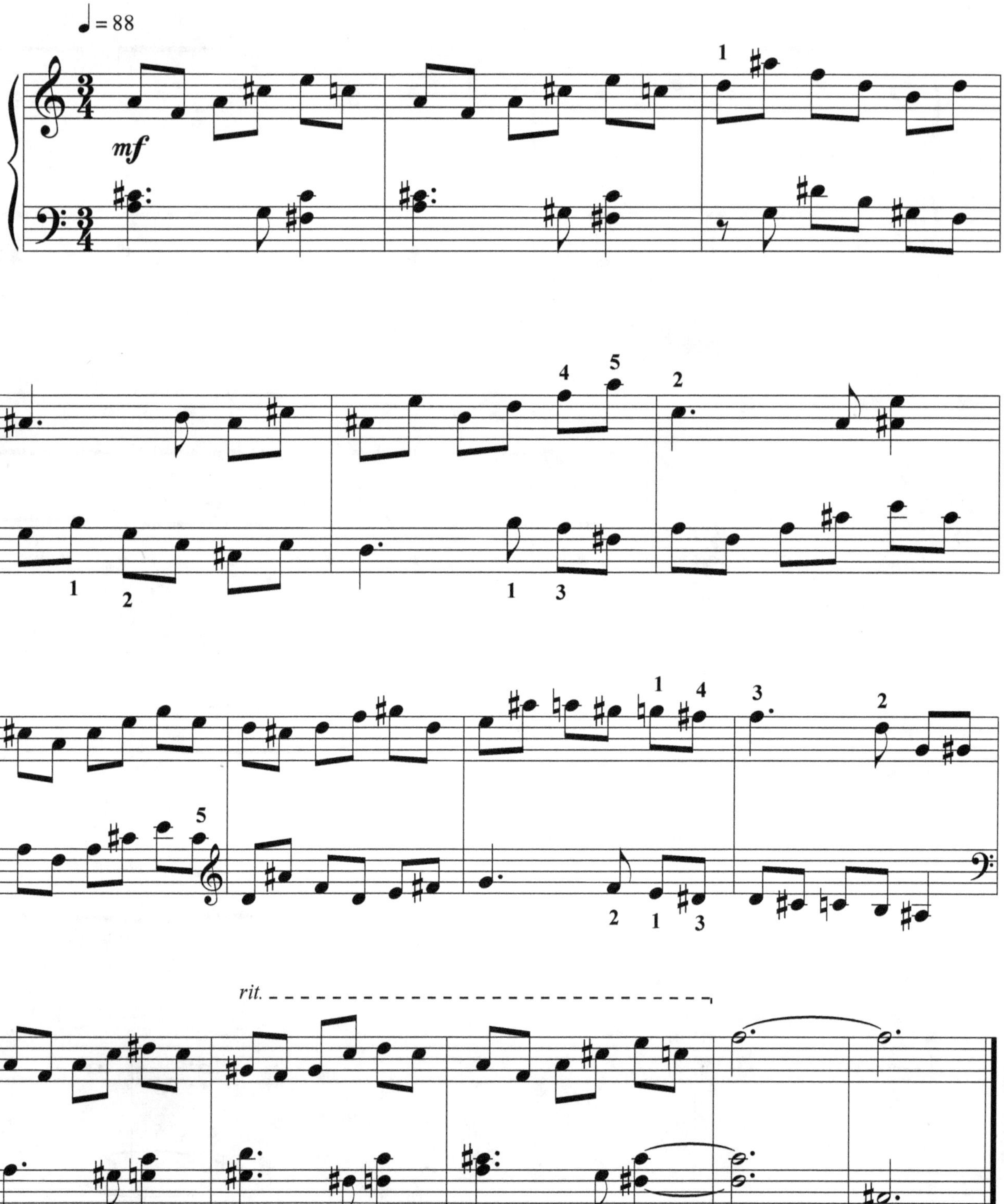

GIVE IT A REST

K.R. ANDERSON

THE CATS WILL PLAY

K.R. ANDERSON

MAKE UP YOUR MIND

K.R. ANDERSON

WIND IT UP

K.R. ANDERSON

YOUR OTHER LEFT

K.R. ANDERSON

FOCUS

K.R. ANDERSON

1234

K.R. ANDERSON

TWENTY-FIVE

K.R. ANDERSON

CAN'T CAN'T CANTER

K.R. ANDERSON

JAN. SESSION

K.R. ANDERSON

CROSS CHOP

K.R. ANDERSON

JUMP RIGHT IN

K.R. ANDERSON

MARCH TO THE OFFBEAT

K.R. ANDERSON

THE CHANGING TIMES

K.R. ANDERSON

PART AND PARCEL

K.R. ANDERSON

LUCKY SEVEN

K.R. ANDERSON

REMEMBER, REMEMBER
(THE 13TH OF DECEMBER)

K.R. ANDERSON

MARCH MACABRE

K.R. ANDERSON

HALF-DOZEN OF THE OTHER

K.R. ANDERSON

SCALING THE WALL

K.R. ANDERSON

DOWN THE ROAD

K.R. ANDERSON

GIVE ME AN "A"

K.R. ANDERSON

COUNT ME OUT

K.R. ANDERSON

HURRY UP

K.R. ANDERSON

DAY IN, DAY OUT

K.R. ANDERSON

CONGREGATION

K.R. ANDERSON

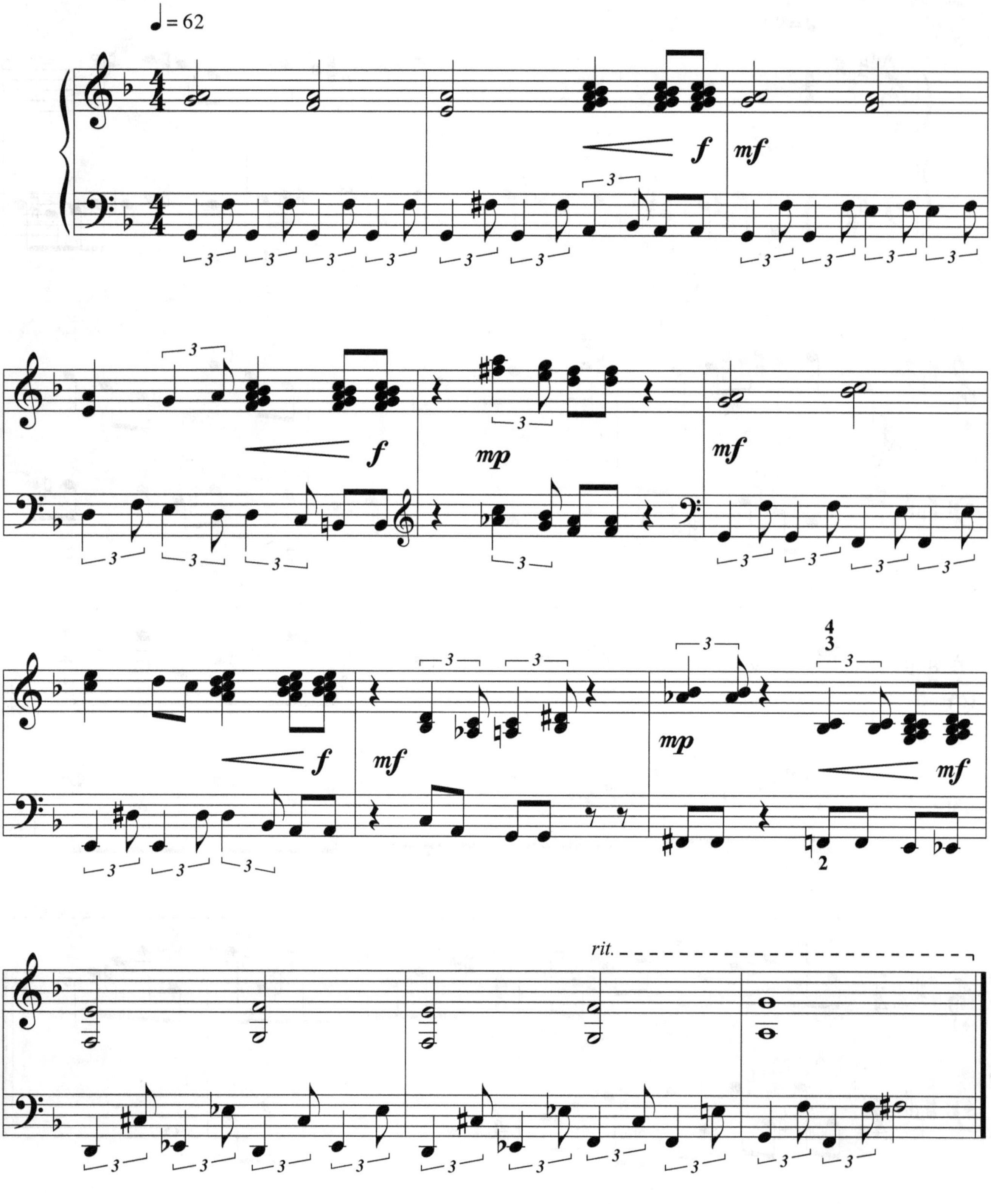

CATCH ME IF YOU CAN

K.R. ANDERSON

BONUS: GRAPHIC MUSIC SCORE

ABOUT

Graphic scores step outside of the established method for notating music; and instead utilize pictures, images or symbols to communicate how the music is to be played. It is a practice that arose during the 1950's and 1960's, and was fueled in part by the idea that standard musical notation was inadequate for expressing the content of certain emerging compositions.

Each graphic score is unique; therefore, how each graphic score is read and played is unique. Unless you are working directly with the composer (which is not uncommon in these cases), the real challenge is often in the interpretation and translation of these symbols into audible music. Even with instruction, the performer will likely have to make unconventional decisions beyond what is required for most musical works.

PLAYING THIS PIECE

In the context of this book, *Precipitation* is less an exercise in traditional sight reading, and more an exercise in interpreting unusual works. Although it would be very unlikely for a performer to be handed a graphic score to perform sight-unseen; the purpose of this exercise is to help sharpen your ability to quickly identify patterns, and to increase your comfort with committing to your intuitive music-making abilities. The more accustomed you become to making quick decisions in uncharted territory, the faster and more confident you'become in other areas as well.

WHAT AM I LOOKING AT?

Take a good look at the page. What is your first impression? Without worrying about specific pitches, imagine what you think the music should sound like from the images on the page. What is the general feeling you get from how the notation is presented?

WHERE DO I START?

Is there an obvious starting or ending point? If not, why not? What's your best guess for the reasons behind that decision? Is looping or repetition noticeably present in the notation, or does it proceed in a simple linear fashion?

How about clefs or notes or tempo? Do you see a pattern? Do you see items that break from that pattern? Use your intuition to guide your decision process.

MAKE A PLAN

Once you have finished examining the page, establish your own guidelines as to how you feel the piece should be played. Commit to the idea of consistency. All similar symbols and groups should follow the same rules at all times.

Then, when you feel confident with your choices, jump right in and play. Don't worry, the water's fine!

Precipitation

K.R. Anderson

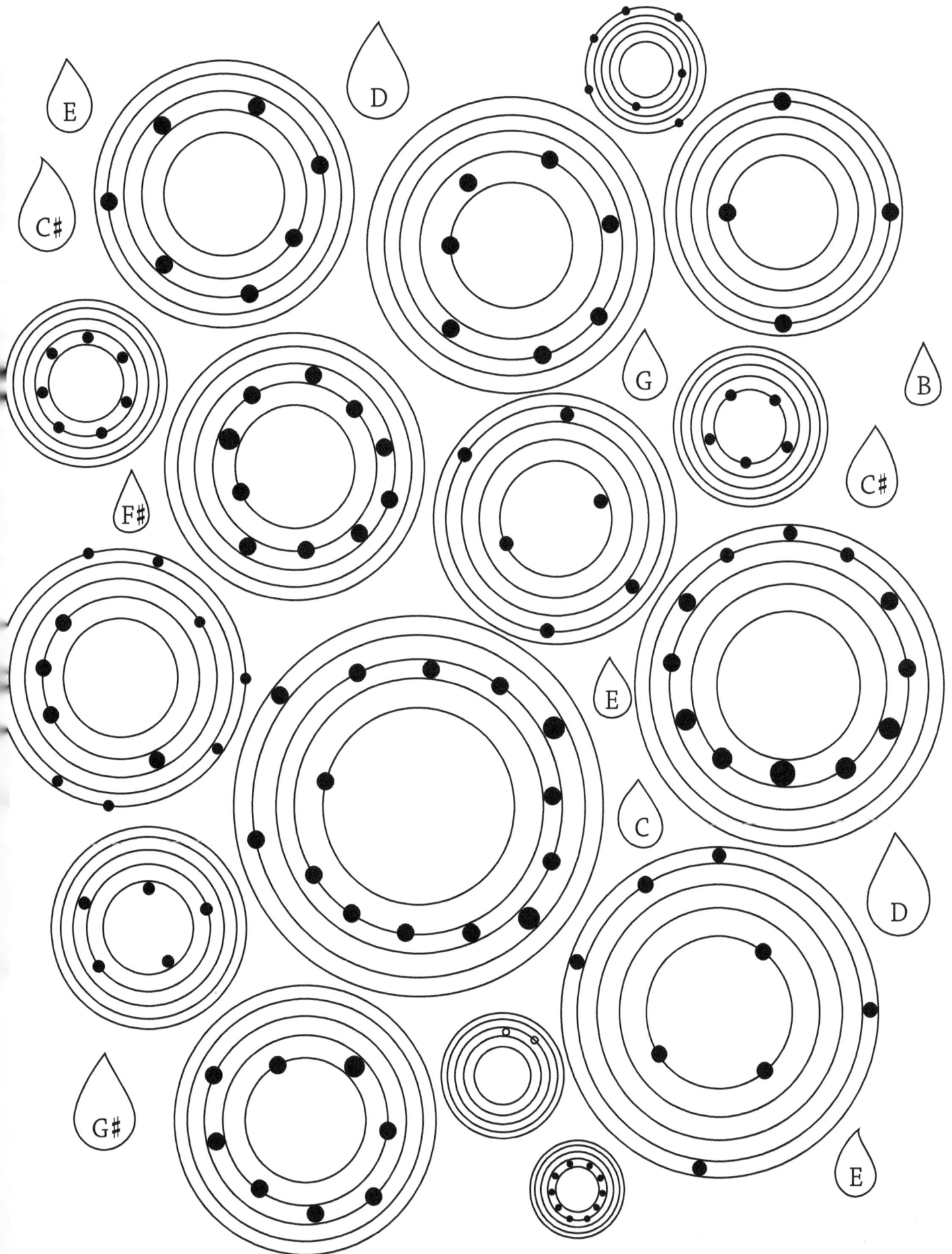

9 780692 451908